Awesome African Animals!

Zebras Are Awesome!

by Megan Cooley Peterson

Consultant: Jackie Gai, DVM
Captive Wildlife Vet

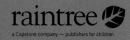
raintree
a Capstone company — publishers for children

Raintree is an imprint of Capstone Global Library Limited, a company incorporated in England and Wales having its registered office at 7 Pilgrim Street, London, EC4V 6LB – Registered company number: 6695582

www.raintree.co.uk
myorders@raintree.co.uk

Edited by Erika Shores and Mari Bolte
Designed by Cynthia Della-Rovere
Picture research by Svetlana Zhurkin
Production by Morgan Walters
Printed and bound in China by Nordica.
0914/CA21401520

ISBN 978-1-406-28849-0
18 17 16 15 14
10 9 8 7 6 5 4 3 2 1

British Library Cataloguing in Publication Data

A full catalogue record for this book is available from the British Library.

Acknowledgements

We would like to thank the following for permission to reproduce photographs: Getty Images: Buena Vista Images, 4—5; Minden Pictures: FLPA/Terry Andrewatha, 25; Newscom: ZUMA Press/Andy Rouse, 23 (middle); Shutterstock: Alexandra Giese, 12—13, Andrzej Kubik, 15 (top), Black Sheep Media (grass), throughout, Chantal de Bruijne, 7, Dmitri Gomon, 8, EcoPrint, 9 (bottom), 26, Eric Isselee, cover (top left, bottom), 11, 32, Francois van Heerden, 18, Harald Toepfer, 21, Hedrus, 16, Joe McDonald, 23 (top), Justin Black, back cover, 24 (top), Karel Gallas, 27, lumen-digital, 9 (top), Muskoka Stock Photos, 19, Pal Teravagimov, 6, sharps, 22—23, Simon_g, cover (top right), 1, 29, Stacey Ann Alberts, 14—15, Stefanie van der Vinden, 17, Steve Allen, 20, Stuart G. Porter, 28—29, SurangaSL (zebra stripes background), back cover and throughout, Villiers Steyn, 10, 24 (bottom)

We would like to thank Jackie Gai, DVM for her invaluable help in the preparation of this book.

Every effort has been made to contact copyright holders of material reproduced in this book. Any omissions will be rectified in subsequent printings if notice is given to the publisher.

All the internet addresses (URLs) given in this book were valid at the time of going to press. However, due to the dynamic nature of the internet, some addresses may have changed, or sites may have changed or ceased to exist since publication. While the author and publisher regret any inconvenience this may cause readers, no responsibility for any such changes can be accepted by either the author or the publisher.

Contents

Striking stripes. 4

Life on the grasslands. 12

Growing up 24

Saving zebras 28

Glossary 30

Books 31

Websites 31

Comprehension questions. 31

Index. 32

Striking stripes

A hungry lion slinks through the tall grass of the savannah. The lion is on the hunt. It spots a group of zebras. The black-and-white stripes of the zebras' coats blend together. The lion cannot pick out a single zebra to chase. It moves on to find easier prey. The zebras are safe for now.

Zebras are mammals famous for their dazzling stripes. Many African animals have brown colouring to blend in with their surroundings. But zebras hide in plain sight. Scientists believe the zebras' stripes break up the outlines of their bodies. Lions, hyenas and cheetahs have trouble telling where one zebra ends and another begins.

There are three types of zebras. Each type has a different stripe pattern. Grevy's zebras have thin, close stripes. Some plains zebras have light brown "shadow stripes" between black stripes. Wide stripes cover a mountain zebra's back. All zebras have black skin under their coats.

Grevy's zebra

plains zebra

mountain zebra

9

Zebras are related to horses and donkeys. Zebras weigh up to 408 kilograms (900 pounds). They can measure up to 1.5 metres (5 feet) tall at the shoulders.

Like horses, zebras have large ears and eyes. A zebra's ears move to hear sounds. Zebras also have excellent vision. At night, a zebra can see as well as an owl!

Life on the grasslands

All wild zebras live in Africa. Grevy's zebras are found in Kenya and Ethiopia. They live on dry grasslands. Plains zebras roam the savannahs and grasslands of eastern and southern Africa. Mountain zebras are found in small areas of Namibia and Angola.

Africa

Where Zebras Live

Zebras live in groups called herds. When there is danger, the herd flees together. Sometimes zebras join herds of giraffes and wildebeests to stay safe.

Zebras work together to keep the herd safe. At night, one zebra stays awake to watch for danger so the rest of the herd can sleep.

Zebras eat for up to 19 hours a day! They munch mostly on grass. They also eat bark, leaves and roots.

A zebra's food does not contain many nutrients.
It has to eat a lot to get the energy it needs.

A zebra's teeth never stop growing. Luckily, all that grazing wears down their teeth.

Teeth also come in handy for scratching and biting. A pair of zebras will clean each other's coats by nibbling them! They also swish away flies with a flick of their tails.

Zebras never travel far from watering holes. They use their hooves to dig for water in dry riverbeds.

20

While drinking, zebras stay on the lookout for predators. Zebras usually drink in the morning when lions are resting.

Zebras use their legs and hooves to stay safe. When in danger, zebras will run away if they can. They can run up to 65 kilometres (40 miles) per hour.

Zebras can also kick predators with their sharp hooves. A single kick from a zebra's back leg can break a lion's jaw.

Growing up

Small family groups make up a zebra herd. Each group has one male zebra, called a stallion. Each family group also includes a few mares and their young, called foals.

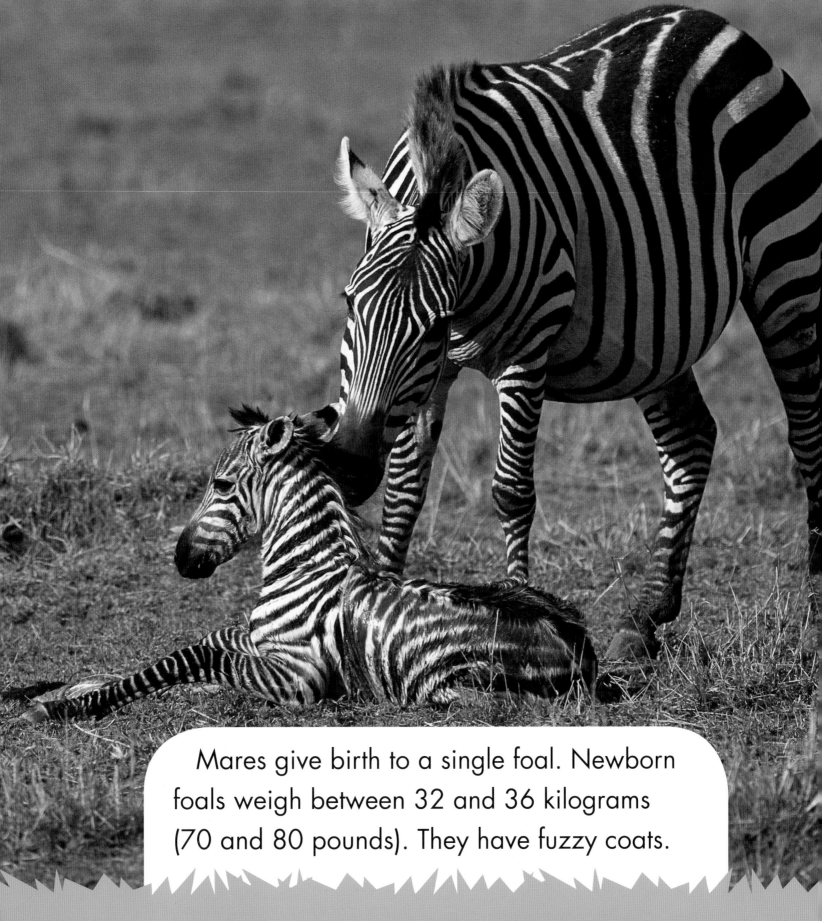

Mares give birth to a single foal. Newborn foals weigh between 32 and 36 kilograms (70 and 80 pounds). They have fuzzy coats.

Foals can walk 20 minutes after birth.
Within an hour they trot along with their
mothers. A foal knows its mother by
her smell and stripes. Each zebra has its
own unique stripe pattern.

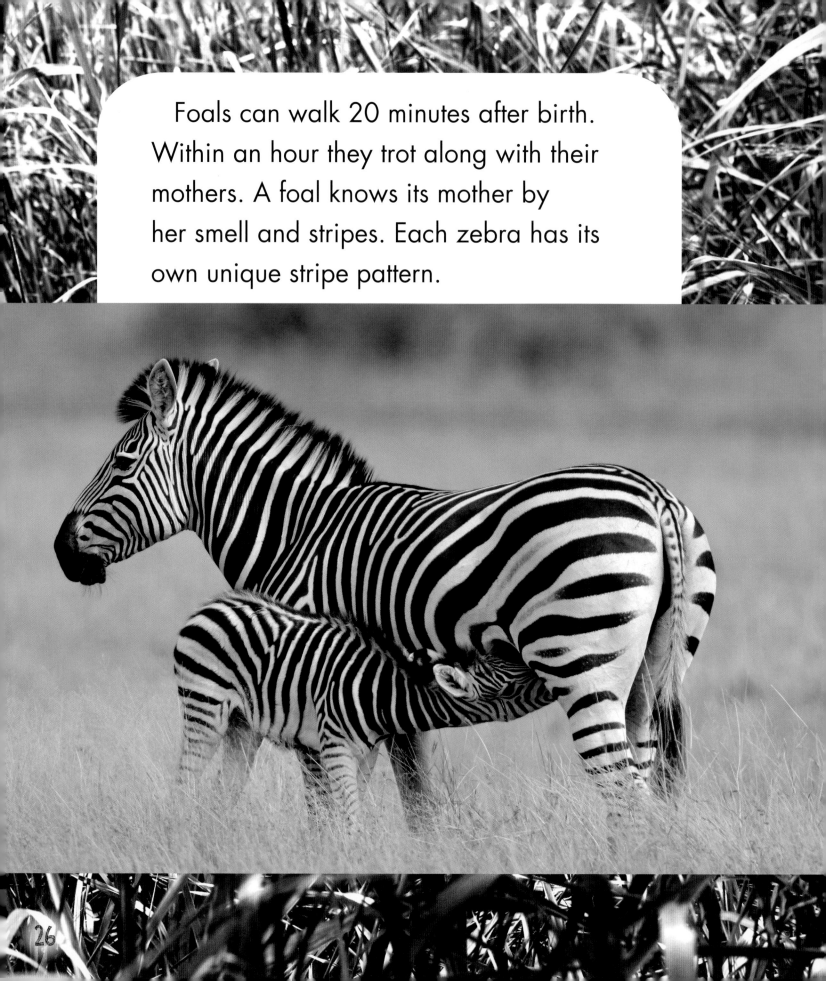

Foals stay close to their mothers for two or three years. In the wild, zebras can live for up to 25 years.

Saving zebras

Some of the land where zebras live has been turned into farms. Zebras are also hunted. Loss of land and hunting has left mountain and Grevy's zebras endangered.

Today people work to protect the land where zebras live. Scientists study zebras to learn how we can help these awesome African animals.

Glossary

endangered in danger of dying out

foal zebra that is less than one year old

grassland large, open area without trees where grass and low plants grow

herd large group of animals that live or move together

hoof hard covering on an animal's foot

mammal warm–blooded animal with hair or fur

mare adult female zebra

nutrient substance that is needed to keep an animal alive and to help it to grow

predator animal that hunts other animals for food

prey animal hunted by another animal for food

savannah flat, grassy area of land with some trees

stallion adult male zebra

unique only one of its kind

Books

Endangered Animals (Eyewitness), Dorling Kindersley (Dorling Kindersley, 2010)

First Encyclopedia of Animals, Paul Dowswell (Usborne Publishing Ltd, 2011)

Websites

http://gowild.wwf.org.uk/regions/africa-games-and-activities/shoe-box-safari
Go wild! Make your own shoebox safari and find out about some more of Africa's amazing animals.

http://www.chesterzoo.org/animals/mammals/horses-and-rhinos/zebra
Find out more about the Grevy's zebra, including the zoo's newest arrival – a zebra foal!

Comprehension questions

1. Describe how a zebra's striped coat protects it from predators.

2. Look at the photos on pages 20–21. Explain why one zebra in both photos is not drinking.

3. How do zebras work together in teams? Why is teamwork important to zebras?

Index

colours 4, 6, 8, 26

foals 24, 25, 26, 27

food 16, 17

habitat 12–13

hearing 11

herds 14, 24

hooves 20, 22, 23

horses 10

life span 27

predators 4, 21, 23

sight 11

size 10, 24

speed 22

teeth 18, 19

types of
    Grevy's 8, 12, 28
    mountain 8, 12, 28
    plains 8, 12